Any

Anywhere

Bruce Meyer

TORONTO

Exile Editions
2000

This edition is published by Exile Editions Limited,
20 Dale Avenue, Toronto, Ontario, Canada   M4W 1K4

Sales Distribution:
McArthur & Company
c/o Harper Collins
1995 Markham Road
Toronto, ON
M1B 5M8
toll free:
1 800 387 0117
(fax) 1 800 668 5788

Layout, Design, and Cover by MICHAEL P. CALLAGHAN
Composed and Typeset at MOONS OF JUPITER, INC. (Toronto)
Printed and Bound by MARC VEILLEUX IMPRIMEUR
Author's Photograph by JOHN REEVES

The publisher wishes to acknowledge
the assistance toward publication of
the Canada Council and the Ontario Arts Council.

The Canada Council
Conseil des Arts du Canada

ISBN 1-55096-536-0

This book is for Kerry, Katie, Carolyn,
Margaret and Homer.

ACKNOWLEDGMENTS:

"Pleiades" and "Threshold" appeared in *Pagitica*, Volume 1, Number 2. My gratitude to the editors for their support.

"Conjunctions" appeared in *I Want To Be The Poet of Your Kneecaps*, edited by John B. Lee and published by Black Moss Press, 1999.

The manuscript for *Anywhere* was runner-up for the 1999 T.S. Eliot Prize.

Thanks to:

Austin Clarke, Ray Robertson, M.T. Kelly, Brian O'Riordan, Julie Roorda, Halli Villegas, H. Masud Taj, David Wevill, Michael Peich and Dana Gioia who responded to the work in this collection and provided excellent feedback;

Fred Addis of the Pier Four, Marine Museum, Toronto, for his professional advice on maritime terminology and for his assistance with historical details for "Noronic;" Jeff Crouch and Leanne Johnston; Dr. Mary Barrie, Lorraine Nishisato, John Rawle and Elise Gervais of the School of Continuing Studies for their encouragement;

and especially Dr. Carolyn Meyer, Margaret Meyer, G. Homer Meyer and Kerry Johnston for their tireless efforts; Michael Callaghan for his intelligent design; and the astute editorial eyes of Molly Peacock, the good maker, who made *Anywhere* come out of nowhere.

Contents

I

A Map of Paradise / 15
The Lovers' Sestina / 16
Subtitles / 18
Twilight / 20
A Hymn Written in Silence to an Unborn Son / 21
As If / 22
Canticle of the Savoir Faire / 24
Pelicans / 26
Good Wine / 27

II

Dinnertime / 30
My Daughter Sleeping / 31
Anywhere / 32
Threshold / 37
The Ferry to South Baymouth / 38
Heaven / 39
Locks / 44
The Honeymoon / 45

III

Mary's Farm / 49
The Office / 50
The City on the Hill / 52
Death and the Human Resources Manager / 56
The Diet / 57
Minors / 58

IV

Conjunctions / 63

Ghazals in the Savannah / 64

Dolphin Watch / 66

Moving / 68

Pleiades / 69

Slipping Away / 71

Noronic / 72

Weeding / 77

Close Reading / 78

Enter In / 79

Night of the Dead / 80

If the Snows Dance / 81

Wind / 82

St. Stephen's Green at Sunrise / 86

It isn't really
Anywhere!
It's somewhere else
Instead!

— A.A. Milne, "Halfway Down"

A Map of Paradise

If I could draw it out in such a way
that would show all the colours
a child might find in a summer's day,
we would make it familiar, forever ours.

That would show all the colours,
the way one looks on something new
we would make it familiar, forever ours.
I would say, *this is as beautiful as you.*

The way one looks on something new —
that tells us a lot about our lives;
I would say, *this is as beautiful as you*
wherever beauty, undying, thrives.

That tells us a lot about our lives,
the suffering we take in stride,
wherever beauty, undying, thrives.
We live the world we want inside.

The suffering we take in stride
proves that paradise is more than faith.
We live the world we want inside
and shape it to a vision of the truth.

This I give you, this map of an anywhere
a child might find in a summer's day
before dreaming becomes a daily dare —
if I could draw it out in such a way.

The Lovers' Sestina

Am I
this song
celebrating you,
each drawn
breath praising
the world?

The world
that I
know, praising
with song,
is drawn
loving you.

Are you
the world
completely drawn,
all I
am, song
for praising?

This praising
that you
call song
is world
enough. I
am drawn,

slowly drawn
to praising
what I
love: you,
the world,
becoming song,

simple song
simply drawn,
a world
where praising
canticles you,
declaring I

am alive, a song of you
drawn from praising
all I know of the world.

Subtitles

for H. Masud Taj

Neither of the twins could remember
how they came to that attic space
or whether they'd been soothed to sleep
by a lullaby at dusk.

They could only remember footsteps,
click of key metal in the lock,
the rush of cold air from the stairwell,
the silence of a nursemaid's hands.

Touching each other on the lips
when they were old enough to talk,
spoke only what the other knew,
naming the world from heartbeats.

Years between them passed in gestures
and their lexicography grew,
became their covenant, their promise,
where every syllable was an hour chimed.

Imagine one year becoming the next,
the attic room growing shorter, smaller;
the hunger to put words to life
found the taste of dawn in sounds.

Their distinguished captor, finished
with his study, declared to his academy
the science of Adam and Eve:
the first language had been Low Dutch;

and showing them the door, the road,
the wind before them almost singing,
they disappeared in their mothered tongue,
a whisper in the night of heaven.

Twilight

for my Father

Between periods as snow fell
and filled the roofless rink,
he'd clear the ice with a shovel
then melt as breath from sight.

In the corners behind mesh
his whispers cheered me on,
the cold upon our flesh
bonding father and son.

On nights of second bests,
the hand on my shoulder was his,
strength in silence silence tests,
love unsparing, all devotion is.

A Hymn Written in Silence to an Unborn Son

If any word should ever reach you,
a message bottled on an uncharted shore,
I would warn you of a truth as true
as the rising sun and certainly more
certain than the seasons of human love
or promising as any promise from above.

I would give you every known word
that might explain what living is —
what weight it is to still be heard
and receive only stone cold echoes
from birdsongs on an August morning
or love's words as they are forming.

And as you are in silence silent now,
so I shall be if ever we should meet.
Tell me with visions across endless snow
in ways not even springtime could repeat —
with saying hands somehow rebuild
the sounds of life that living willed.

Bruce Meyer

As If

As if I am tired of speaking of grand passion
        and find instead a sustaining happiness;

as if you were to turn to me in the night
        and speak through my sleeplessness of love;

as if I were to imagine the sea inside my head
        and for a calm instant build a nest for us there;

as if by miracle our garden suddenly awoke
        and the snow blossomed in a flood of impatiens;

as if we stand by our child's crib as she dreams
        and promise her tomorrows we won't know ourselves;

as if I were to find in you the source for all
        my metaphors that hold the world together;

as if my journey were of no purpose than to return
        to you and tell you of great adventures;

as if our footprints on the tide's new palimpsest of sand
        were not washed away by the ebb and flow;

as if I told you in a quiet moment that we
        should not be afraid because we dream;

as if the rocks jutting into the surf were really a signal
        that something remains after we lose count of days;

as if all the suffering of history and memory
      could equal the power of one thought of truth;

as if I am tired of seeking grand passion
      and find instead a sustaining happiness;

as if you were to turn to me in the night
      and speak through my sleeplessness of love;

we could say to the world *you may believe in life again,*
      it is everywhere you breathe; it lives in simple wishes.

Canticle of the Savoir Faire

for Austin Clarke

The bulls and the bears go dancing
to prey on the life of the field,
but isn't it all enhancing
when they garner a windfall yield?

They bid on the tides of the ocean,
they barter for futures and pasts
and with a merchant commotion
unleash their profited blasts.

Come trip with them on the midway,
come try your hand at a chance,
ride the wheel up the long way,
and never lose step with the dance.

For the calliope music is avid,
and horses chase daylight in bonds,
there's a mine in Malaysia that's loaded
and a rumour that's hot among friends —

welcome to where a buck is a buck
and the buzzards circle the kill —
it's feeding time and the bull's in luck
as the knights of gold test their skill.

It's in the averages, the favorite game,
the measure is indexed with pride,
but will it ever be the same
when the sharks go out with the tide?

The heads will dizzy and dazzle,
the corks will pop for the feast,
until the day of the fizzle
and kingdom's the prey of the beast.

The knights will hide in their closets,
the Jacks will come tumbling down,
and the silent kings who rule regrets
will send out a champion Clown.

He'll stand at the cross-roads of commerce,
he'll wave a sword in its rust,
and somehow manage to coerce
a handful of dreams from the dust.

For always the wizards of fortune
stand apart from the rage of the storm,
their know-how as pure as a winter moon,
their wealth kept off-shore and warm.

And soon the carnies and barkers
will raise the tent from the soil.
The kingdom again will go starkers
and the pot go back on the boil.

With the bulls and the bears let's go dancing,
to prey on the life of the field,
with some savoir-faire we'll be chancing
a shot at a windfall yield.

Pelicans

for my Mother

Look in their yellow, prehistoric eyes.
The surf sounds like a heart beating;
the fog is blowing off, the skies
will soon glisten and begin to sing.

The surf sounds like a heart beating.
My child entering the green ocean
will soon glisten and begin to sing.
She is entranced by the constant motion.

My child entering the green ocean —
a first time for everything under the sun.
She is entranced by the constant motion,
the strange power that makes things run.

A first time for everything under the sun:
a first kiss, a first night, a small forever,
the strange power that makes things run
in a world where each thing finds another,

a first kiss, a first night, a small forever,
the tide against the pearl-white sands
in a world where each thing finds another
like pelicans paired in marriage bands.

The tide against the pearl-white sands
is whispering its desire to the shore,
like pelicans paired in marriage bands —
the old hunger of the world wants more.

Good Wine

Let me believe you are April light,
the ghost in the vineyard waking up,

an earthy spirit dancing delight,
the first and last drop in my cup.

Dinnertime

Behind the screen a figure moves,
an old woman in rolled white hair,
hands busied with a wooden spoon —
she pauses as if searching for a word:
who is going to tell the boy?

He bends to pick a windfall up,
turning the discovery in his hand
and one by one, the shadows wait,
the story waits; the boy is young.
He smells the aroma of dinner cooking.

The door opens and he is called.
And what if he forgets the garden,
loses the taste of that seasoned dish,
the smell of apples against his cheek,
a patch of earth beneath the boughs?

There'll be that bed where he counted stars,
its metal frame as cold as death,
skeins of clothes hung on pegs,
the parlour clock sounding ten,
counting the seconds of a broken heart.

My Daughter Sleeping

sighs with the softness
of snow falling on snow,
infant, silent stars
afloat on indigo;

whispers secrets, says
what dreaming dares —
bud of a new rose,
sunrise haloed in soft hairs .

Anywhere

The future stands still, dear Mr. Kappus, but we move
in infinite space.
> —Rainer Marie Rilke, *Letters to a Young Poet*

1)

...And when he came out
the universe had changed.
The styles were different,
the kids listened to music
that sounded like machines.
His friends had grown old.
All the great possibilities
resembled outdated diaries,
the same story but new words.
The years no longer matched.
Conversations lay in shards.
The trees had grown taller,
and his name had an echo.
The sensation of sudden falling
while standing still as law.
He could go anywhere, anywhere
his thoughts led him now,
further than the ninety paces
the yard had once allowed;
but even that was too far.
Anything his heart desired
was a meal without taste —

the swallowing was harder
like sinking stones in a pond
or poems that opened doors
and graves left best at peace.

2)

By morning, as the shadows azured
and the sequins turned to diamonds
in the clear bright air, she fumbled
into her coat and boots, and calling, assured
her mother she was dressed and found
a patch, deep blue and undisturbed

in the open field. There she lay down.
The first sensation a slap on her neck
that soon went numb. The sky above,
almost endless, opened to own
her as small wings spread to break
earth's grip, short of angelic love.

3)

Was it low mist over the ripe fields
or the green light of the horizon
as the sun set in a band of pine
that made him stop the car and watch —

the air motionless, momentarily, everything
standing still to listen. He took two
steps, then quickened his pace. Frogs
leapt from wet grass, his pantlegs

darkened as spur weed like obligations
tugged and pleaded at his ankles —
and at the fence, the soft-eared mulleins
waved good-bye as he walked on and on

then disappeared from sight. Anywhere.
Anywhere. He left no footprints.

4)

Though you were too young to remember
the autumn sunlight on city streets,
pavement strewn with fallen leaves,
your mother and I went shopping,
bought a teapot, made sandwiches
and listened for the herald pain
that became a symphony by dusk.
The night became slow and silent
and the hushed corridors shone
with phrases of antiseptic secrets.
I gazed into the closed courtyard
at lighted windows in the long shaft
and thought, *there is dying here,*
there is much, too much, to know.
And when your heartbeat vanished,
a voice in the night grown mute,
it was as if the hour was forever —
the panic deep inside your universe,
your apprehension needing comfort;
yet you came to us at daybreak,
a breath or hapless cry for help,
the music of the monitors like spheres
said *I am here, wherever I am,*
receive me, love me, be my guide.
The corridor became a street again
crowded with morning business,
as the starched white linen light
wrapped you tightly in its bond,
saying *Once upon a time in a place*
that could be anywhere, a little girl
drew breath, and her parents named her...

Threshold

The house wasn't really empty, was it.
The rooms, their carpets marked by other
people's tables, brown cartons split
open like realizations, and another
and another item on the list of dreams,
emptied me. That moving day now seems

to stand still, as still as you standing
there, your back turned to the doorway
of our new house. The light flooding
the disheveled yard struggled to say
*This is your life now, this shell found
in the wrack. Fill it with your sound.*

I slowly put my ear to this life...
the voice of our daughter crying to come
to us, your waking sighs, my wife,
that greet me each dawn. *This is home,*
said my heart as you turned in the light.
Come in. Speak of love. Say it right.

The Ferry to South Baymouth

My daughter's eyes are blue as Georgian Bay
and sparkle with the glint of tiny stars
that define each wave on a summer's day;

for among the vacationers who have run away
with all their necessities packed in cars,
my daughter's eyes are blue as Georgian Bay.

This is her first summer. She has a way
of measuring things as her eye explores
and defines each wave on a summer's day

with the luxury of unencumbered sight. I say
boat but all she sees are endless waters —
my daughter's eyes are blue as Georgian Bay.

Her little hand points to a gull, the sway
and lilt of its wings on wind. All that matters
as she defines each wave on a summer's day

and sparkles with the glint of tiny stars
is that she is fed and dry and happily ours —
my daughter's eyes are blue as Georgian Bay
and define each wave on a summer's day.

Heaven

I hurt at the sight of the familiar,
the strain of seeing past happiness revived
in a momentary image so distant, so far
only its living light survived.

Every man must have his heaven,
a seed pearl sewn near the heart —
mine was the summer of sixty-seven,
a postage-stamp beach that stood apart

from pillars of fire in the daily news.
Boston. Detroit. Chicago. L.A. —
all the ashes were circling curlews
as time held its breath for a single day

and the Sound's current repeated its churning:
off in the distance Providence is burning.

It must be taken with a grain of salt
though it was just a holiday moment,
a footprint on the sands, a somersault...
the world never righted; a warm current

in the cold flow headed for open sea.
My grandparents sit on saran chairs,
my sister digs down to the watery
in-flood of an old tide — this was theirs

and mine, a peace in a world fraught
with its own dismay, that little beach,
the windmill at its end. I am not
certain it is still within my reach.

Heaven is a tithe on life's earning —
off in the distance Providence is burning.

It was frightening for a child to watch time fly,
my arms and legs lengthening, days growing short;
standing at the water's edge I wondered if to die
meant knowing what dark and distant port

lay beyond the horizon's line, beyond Nantucket
and the Gulf Stream's current,
wondering what the dead learn and the living forget,
and seeing my pale toes as I bent

to touch a shell in the jumbled backwash
where things are never sorted out.
Returning to that one instant I dash
the pain life taught me and roll it in a shout

only to find what the world keeps learning:
off in the distance Providence is burning.

I am terrified of losing respect for truth;
losing the ability to recall the sea stench
wracked at ebb upon sands, uncertain proof
that high-tide storms could wrench

life from life and reduce it to a trinket
for a castle gate, a prize I could find
and lay at my parents' feet; I have yet
to find anything of equal worth. I remind

myself that illusions carry me forward,
that only love and promises can cope
with the tides of desire as I fall toward
the real heaven so far beyond this hope,

daft in its love, in its beautiful yearning.
Off in the distance Providence is burning.

Remember the morning after the storm,
the beach strewn with lifeless debris.
Wild, pale boys gathered in a swarm
around a dead nurse shark. I could see

its eyes searching the sky in vague praise,
the look of staring into the night stars
and wondering if God in all His mysteries
was watching from His glory. Ours

the kingdom here, the power, the persuasion,
the footprint at the sea's edge begging
for the wash to stay at bay, the occasion
when it might and the tide reneging

on its promise. Let the world keep turning.
Off in the distance Providence is burning.

I think I should reconsider heaven.
It is a sad place full of the joy that sadness
brings. It is the helping that comes to leaven
the loaf. It is the sustenance that once

consumed cannot be shared — a private place
that, in the center of the heart, even God
would find too small to inhabit. I trace
the path of a single grain of sand, that odd

missing piece of a child's tentative castle
as it bakes and falls in the midday sun —
the light of grace, its very weight, conceals
all the patience of eternity in one

thought, the doubt of its own discerning.
Off in the distance Providence is burning.

Only its living light has survived.
I cling to that faint hope like a castaway
sunburnt on the shore of a place that thrived
and disintegrated long ago, leaving the dismay

of tangled ruins for the hopeful to weep in.
Ah, promises, promises. Let's strike a covenant.
I will grant You a love greater than sin
and You, You will sit silent, indifferent

yet watchful, a handful of sea and sky
in Your pocket, ready to create another illusion
that may be more beautiful than the last. I
will bear Your light. I have my heaven.

Its message is starlight that arrives still burning:
off in the distance Providence is burning.

Locks

> *for Katie*

Someday I shall tell you how fine
a child you were, how your soft hair
in my hand stilled the flow of time —
> *where does the river go from there?*

Oaks of Merrickville stood watch,
the Rideau rippled sluice and shore,
wide I opened my arms to catch —
> *where will the river go from there?*

Light through the trees was golden,
as blond and brilliant as your hair,
or small laughter. Your face shone.
> *How far does the river go from there?*

Simple songs are hardest sung,
where light braves shadows on a dare —
never forget that you were young:
> *The river runs from there.*

Look beyond the bending. Boats
disappear in the reeds. I share
your song of life, its few spare notes...
> *Will we follow the river from here?*

Shall I ask innocence to be
the guardian of places where
we find happiness? O tell me:
> *where does the river go from there?*

The Honeymoon

> *"Slowly I turned...step by step...inch by inch..."*

A beginning contains so much of what
the marriage is, the power of all that
water pouring and pouring its happiness
over the brink, and promise after promise
leaving the lips until you think *where
did that come from* and *can I care
enough to make a life out of words?*
Applause in church was like startled birds.

We started up Clifton Hill, the Falls
behind us roaring with what she calls
all that nature trying to mean something,
and that weird street twisted and writhing
like an animal in pain, the bridal chamber
of horrors sandwiched between the clamour
of the beer garden and the Pizza Hut: our
love nest. Imagine making love for an hour

while someone plays mini-putt just yards
away. I don't know what's in the cards
for us. This place is like a dream that was
used and thrown away; the good shoes
too good to wear every day; the face of an old
chambermaid, lined from tugging soiled
sheets as if living for those impossible,
mad-eyed dreamers swept in the wash of it all.

Mary's Farm

for Mary and Andy Barrie

is seated atop a winding road
where hill crest almost touches clouds
and summer shadows all blow by
away from the city's crowds;

is a place remade, a place of ghosts,
of laughter's thirst and saddened wind
where old door hinges sing to time
because they've found a friend;

is guarded by swallows and water nymphs
who sing of pastures and silent barns,
a melody as soft as milkweed down
of how each season turns;

is patterned on decades of daisy chains
and memories of each season's cost,
but balanced by praises of singing larks,
by what is, but isn't lost;

is gilded with Victorian gingerbread
where an eave of gothic crowning parts;
on Mary's farm where time stands still
the Muses work their arts;

is somewhere made by dreaming hard,
is somewhere in the work-day's crush,
the neverland that never cried —
listen now, deep inside. Hush.

The Office

At the washroom door two secretaries
wonder aloud if today will be the day
the list comes down. The functionaries
have been meeting and the talkers say
the decision is coming. A lone telephone
sings to itself somewhere down the floor
and desktops like landing lights alone
on a foggy runway glare along the corridor.

Jane has been here seven years, has three
kids to look after. Meg is barely new.
Two years doesn't count for much. To be
honest, no one seems safe. It's just do
one's job and quietly hope for the best.
The hushed voices from cubicles sound
like waves upon a shore, repeat and rest
and fling back upon the shaky ground
of grey hard-twist and ergonomic chairs.

Sendel from accounting knows the score.
He's seen the spread-sheets from upstairs
and knows this quarter has seen more
red than a bull at a matador's feet.
He staples the list together and slowly
calculates his way to the bulletin board
beside the staff lounge on the second.

No long, toasted good-byes, just collapsible
banker boxes and paper bags, few fond
parting remarks as Security responsible
for quick exits ushers the named-ones out
and the taxis pull away.

               This afternoon
it is kind outside. The spring day is hot.
It might feel good to be free again
where the pavement throws up a light
so brilliant one could almost tan by it.
That is what time means — the sight
of people waiting by newsstands, wait
and think and wait again.

               Sendel's fast
glance just to make sure as the thumb
tack penetrates the cork and the last
detail is in place. He hears the hum
of discussion as the bodies gather to read
the names aloud; and then the silence.

In all the empty cubicles where the dead
once toiled each day...a little recompense
settles like a dust upon the waiting shelves.
Today, considers one survivor, *I was not
the one. Tomorrow? Count yourselves
lucky. Work goes on. Give it your best shot.*

The City on the Hill

for M.T. Kelly

The car steals up to the curbside
under the cover of darkness, and rain
that would find the life inside

a lost kernel of black maize falls again
on a city hungry for another spring.
Broadview Avenue has much to explain,

and time, that old enemy of everything,
flashes in the rearview mirror and breaks
the spell of a continuous story longing

to be told. And so our history speaks.
It speaks in the windows of old
houses where the last light leaks

into the night like run-off, where bold
whispers of what was challenge the sky
with silhouettes of what is, the untold

stories of the Toronto that cannot die
though buried and forgotten, left
for rubbish or seekers of curiosity

who idle their cars on a spring night
as the rain falls on a silent, ancient
place where lives are lived right

on top of the past and the past, spent
and wearied with its own living,
quietly says *get on with it*. I went

to the Archives and found the unforgiving
silence of the future in the sepias
and faded greys, in the hand-tinting

of triptychs and never-built replicas
of a grander world that could have
happened here; and the small trivias

of what was and was not could prove
only what I thought might be possible,
so leave it at that. Loving the past is to love

what might become of the future —
a city on the hill rising up from the Don,
sixty thousand lives running on the pure

necessity of survival — Teiaiagon,
the Iroquois called it, its palisaded
walls like laws in the City codes, on

and on, with details that could have persuaded
Aquinas to simplicity. The bones resting
beneath Withrow Public School, jaded

slightly by the changes above but testing
the patience and reserve bones are known
to possess, might flash an answer, guessing

at what the question is, practicing to hone
a haunting in the Boys' toilet or there,
high in the empty boughs or the cone

of some replanted pine. It makes a whisper
as if the trees can talk, saying to a child
you are in my footsteps, be sure, be sure.

Last night the moon was full and wild,
its aura drowned out the stars politely
apologizing for the bright and haloed

magnificence that is the world's one dignity.
Some things don't change. The light
from distant stars is only arriving now. See?

There in the twinkling of an eye, right
before us as if we needed proof, is history.
Imagine the rest, but give it the light

to find its own way in its own verity.
The future always troubles the truth,
so let's make it simple. Let's just say

the rain, the moon, the proof
is there, and once high in the city
on the hill the wind danced with

the dreamer to the rhythm of the rain,
and that was enough, in all the pain
and suffered ignorance, to steal life again,

and place it by the fire in birch basket
where the smoke blinded the eye yet
made a vision too powerful to forget.

Death and the Human Resources Manager

It came slowly like a morning memo
or a burst of corporate inspiration.
The telephone rang. The rolodex, slow
to respond, offered no networking.
It was as if the entire operation
had been outsourced. He was asking

a question at the time. The answer
had something to do with attrition,
an overlooked redundancy. Sure
of its legalities, the silence battled
to be heard. That was how policy
came down. The matter settled,
Life went out to lunch with Reality.

The Diet

for Barry Callaghan

Living a little seems like dying slow.
Living a lot is better than dying slow.
    Let's have more of everything before we have to go.

Loving a little is preferred to dying slow.
Loving a lot and you forget you're dying slow.
    Babe, let's do something before we have to go.
    Let's have more of everything before we have to go.

Needing a little feels like dying slow.
Needing a lot is the same as dying slow.
    Let's have more of everything before we have to go.
    O Babe, let's do it all before we have to go.

Dying a little is better than living slow.
Dying a lot is just like living slow.
    Don't say I didn't warn you. Now it's time to go.

Minors

Light drained from the steel mesh cage.
Men, listen up, he heard through the stink
of wet leather and sweat-soaked pads
hanging like double overtime in the room.
This is how the condemned face truth —
the large trusting eyes of young boys
still wide with possibilities and dreams...
the following people have made the team.

What was it he saw in the purple glow
of the streetlamped sky that night?
His tied skates slung over his stick,
the snow-cold slowly eating its way
through the husky socks and rubber boots
that bulged over shin pads held by elastics.
The faint yellow stars rode his back,
the snows parted, not wishing to be near.

His footsteps turned away from home,
tracking across the unbroken blue
of a field that led to the town's ravine.
An ice-crust, half-eaten on the river,
lay broken like rules or simple longings;
it held him a short while, long enough
to hear the current roar like a crowd,
the visitors a goal ahead...he took the ice.

Where had his footprints gone by spring?
Where was the breath that curled in the air
and the godly magic of December dreams?
The taste of ice in a young boy's mouth,
the taste of ice from a player's blades
is cooling, soothing and suddenly sharp,
numb as two minutes frozen in time.
Someday, he'd vowed, *I'll skate with the stars.*

Conjunctions

for Kerry

The parts of speech rattle through our lives,
the fret of prepositions driving us to do,
the nouns we wear as husbands and wives,
and verbs which live on after us as you

flip through the pages of dusty albums —
what became of us so quickly, how time flies.
What is it holds us together as the seasons
disappear like earnings and each garden dies?

Let me find you in the grammar of desire.
Let me touch you in those shank hours when
there are no words, only hopes, when the fire
that cannot be quenched says *begin again*

and the syntax that drives our being forms
like frost on a window pane, so beautifully,
so silently, drawing us and tracing patterns —
with, yet, and — this joining for all eternity.

Bruce Meyer

Ghazals in the Savanna

1)

I pick you a wildflower. In this lace
of white tapestry I find breathing space.

Do you notice how the restless birds race
against the wind yet never fall from grace?

Take my hand. Let us explore the commonplace
and find passion in the things we praise.

It is summer again. The creatures pace
in their wilderness and slowly we embrace.

The high grass is wet with dew as I trace
the outline of the morning in your face.

2)

I want to imagine Africa as a mystery
that fills the night with an aching liberty.

In the darkness, half dreaming, I accidentally
touched your hand and plead uncertainty.

Outside our window the night wept bitterly
and no one measured its pain or dignity.

And when we woke before dawn to see
the stars fade, those birds sang in the tree.

That is how the dew settled. Small grassy
arms reached up to comfort you and me.

Nature knows more of suffering than we
will ever guess. Life is everlasting, patiently.

Can you picture the age-old migratory
paths of temporal creatures tired and thirsty?

The dark continents of our imaginations shall be
waiting for us. Let all the animals run free.

Bruce Meyer

Dolphin Watch

Tonight as I look into the setting sun,
the dolphins seem almost proliferate —
their black shapes arching with one
perfect motion through the temperate
aqua-green dusk as if to anticipate
a resurrection, a signal of the way
one hopes for things with great
desire only to find them another day.

Yesterday on the dolphin watch, one
sought the creatures with a zeal
large enough to make for a let-down
when none were seen. They migrate
to the deeper waters; we were late
in the season on the lifeless bay.
Inevitability said *this is your fate;
desire only to find them another day.*

The red sinking sun has a question:
what is it that you want? The long wait,
like a promise of some resurrection
is almost given up when out there, a late-
comer, a straggler's dark-finned silhouette
appears just as I was about to turn away,
the clue to a mystery, an insatiate
desire only to find them another day.

Maybe God still loves the world, and late
in the story of creation He has begun
to enjoy what hope does, that great
desire only to find them another day.

Moving

The last box gone, the open door,
a jetsam of chairprints on the floor,
and with a touch of empty grief
comes the going without relief
and then, no more.

For all the pleasures of the place
are picture stains of sunlit trace,
and as an echo fades away
you cannot grasp what you cannot say:
this was commonplace.

Here is the latchkey to leave behind.
Here are the papers checked and signed.
Open the closet for one last time
as skeletal hangers touch and chime,
their arms entwined.

You were always certain this was home,
a place where you could always come...
refurnish it within the mind,
pretend it was not left behind,
empty and lonesome.

Where will we be in another year?
Is it memory that insists on fear
of tomorrows the mind cannot invent?
Time is time wherever it is spent,
but just not here.

Pleiades

The wind is awake tonight.
The chance of blooding only happenstance
for mosquitoes and the blackflies.

George Grant, not long ago,
wondered where we stood in time,
withdrew from the roar of centuries,

and suddenly, leaving us cold,
pronounced us a nation without stars.
They fall and none lament.

The ancients used to steer by them,
knew the world from what they said,
and they spoke to them of limits.

Ah love, what's the bloody use —
this is where we are and none
are going to cite us for our glory.

Heaven's miracle is its renewable resource —
the light it cannot spend tonight
will be saved for tomorrow and remade

like so much water, like so much rock,
and we see tails drawn against the dark
like lines crossed out upon a page

where something better is always possible
before it exceeds our grasp
and falls to earth as heaven's rage.

Slipping Away

Like the smell of lavender in a room
where the over-painted radiator
kept the temperature due north,
the aroma of roast beef lingering
like a conversation downstairs...

I would open the heavy walnut drawer,
secretly, as if a ghost,
and slipping my hand between the silks
and smoothing a slightly rumpled scarf
stare into the distance of those eyes.

She was a handsome woman.
Hair piled and neatly pinned behind,
the sadness in the smile-lines developed
of waiting for the shutter to release,
the easy death of a moment in that room.

Everything had not been worn in years;
the satin belt like arms wrapped in love;
and for one last unconnected glance
the pince-nez through which she saw a light;
the fox-wrap and its hungering heads.

Noronic

These words are the stark cold water
poured upon the still glowing embers
of some one hundred and nineteen lives.
These words, in the end, matter
little. They say only, someone remembers,
someone too distant to know the heat,
the smell of metal screaming hot,
the stench of the CNE morgue. This survives
because one hundred and nineteen did not.

Let's sift through the artifacts, the stories.
Here is a Yankee nickel, the tailed head
of Thomas Jefferson still pointing the way
to democracy: it is one of the memories,
blackened by heat, fused with a bead
of silver on its rim. It came from the tuck-
shop on the *Noronic*, welded to a muck
of valueless weight, the currency of the day
being paid in grief, frustration and bad luck.

It hadn't always been tragic, the *Noronic*;
there had been the laughter and gaiety
of countless summer cruises, sunlight
sparkling off the bright waters and scenic
passages as far from the final tragedy
as a mind can imagine. And each spring,
a fresh coat of heavy white paint layering
the rails and screens made her bright
for another year of smooth lake sailing.

But had she been jinxed from the start?
On her maiden voyage in nineteen thirteen,
almost a year after the *Titanic* went down,
she proved unstable, heeling to port
from her superstructure and certain unseen
forces. It had its spirit and a spirit takes
its presence from the untrustworthy lakes,
then frees it as if it were never its own.

But *Noronic* would not give it back —
welding its name to a place, Pier Nine
of Toronto Harbour, gripping an autumn
night in the middle of a century. Look
it up in the newspapers and design
a plaque to commemorate the event:
the spirit refuses to let go. It is bent
on its own course and running fast from
a late summer squall, slows, hesitant,

until it reaches a deadly, idle still.
It had rained hard early on that cruise,
a cold front settling in, sending the season
into the dark recess of time where an ill
wind blew through the portholes with news
of an unexpected change — the currents
warmed by August still laughingly intent
on a good time and the last liaison
to July revelling against the portent

of winter. Past Detroit and Cleveland,
slipping beyond Buffalo by dusk, the pristine
lights of Pt. Abino glistened on the surface,

the final moments of giddiness in grand
style shipped with her — the solemn green
of Ontario's silt ran eagerly beneath her
all the way to Toronto, and with the closure
of the bar, marked its arrival at its place
alongside Pier Nine, presumably secure.

My father and my uncle crewed for years,
earning their college fees, passing the bellhop's
uniform like a hand-me-down among
the family. And coming through the Gap, cheers
would ring from decks as moor lines dropped,
caught cold-handed by stevedores. The rush
to get ashore at sunset and disappear in the crush
of Yonge Street was the highlight. A few hung
back, drinking privately to the lapping hush

of harbour waters on *Noronic's* hull —
most would go ashore to see their families
or spend American dollars like water
in the taverns and restaurants and dull
night spots the city was known for. *Seize
the moment* was the motto of the lake trade.
Holidaying families and surreptitious couples made
strange shipmates. In the end it didn't matter.
They were bound together. Their fates laid.

Many had returned to their cabins by midnight.
The last dance had played, a soft melody,
the strains flowing from the afterdeck,
the harbour reflecting each decorative light,

the moment almost perfect. A car along the Quay,
a few partygoers talking in the dark, the gangway
saying *come to bed, there will be more play*
tomorrow...come rest your head on Noronic.
And so ended the last summer day.

It was one-thirty. Someone heard a crackling
in a closet. A porter was summoned. A key
kept elsewhere. An alarm was late being rung.
The Captain ashore was late returning.
Eleven minutes later, the ship was a sea
of living flames. The corridors turned black,
the air so hot and thick made one choke
as hands fought their way ahead to be stung
by the very walls and floors that spoke

so graciously of ease only an hour before.
The city sky lit up with a bright orange glow,
the whistle in a breathless note sounding
a shroud of pain and despair — and on shore
the witnesses watching grown men throw
small children in the slip. Some fought
their way down ropes as the fire fighters
streamed water on the decks, cannonading
through portholes, sizzling to steam on the hot

steel plates of the hull. Stories said she groaned
and shuddered all the way to Hamilton where
they broke her up for scrap; complained to the last
as if the spirit in her had somehow found
another wind, a cyclone in the dead of winter

turning back upon itself. The last artifact
is the headlines, the papers of account and fact
that fall silent and yellow, lost in the past.
The stars are dead cold in the final act,

and these words, tears poured upon an ember,
cool the story enough so someone will remember.

Weeding

Whenever light falls in the open patches,
bleaching the earth's secrets to a bone,
the spark of green ignites and catches
to scintillate the tinder in the stone.

Some shoots are delicate, small, fine
limbs that ballet softly toward open sky,
blossoming, crossing that green line
between unloved growth and beauty.

Life, even unwanted, will always find
a way. Beneath the order lurks a need,
unbridled passion defying shape and kind —
turn your back for a week, it goes to seed.

I pluck it out now, the roots screaming
at the open air, grey fingers in channels
torn from their indifferent dreaming
and tossed in a withered heap as charnels.

Close Reading

In the bedroom's morning light
my infant daughter and my wife
softly study each other's faces.

I ask if anything can be more right
than knowing what love is to life,
the meaning one word embraces.

Enter In

to honour the wedding of Ivan McFarlane

I will never stand outside your window
on a rainy night or listen to the sound
of my heartbeat without yours in-tow —
I will never enter an empty room or find
a shell in the wind-smoothed sands
without wondering at how your voice
could fill it with desire. Our hands
now joined in clapping raise a noise
that awakens you in me and me in you.

If the truth be known, and I know it will,
then let me say that in everything I do
you enter in. Imagine how I can tell
the morning light about finding your door.
Come in, said Love. *I will give you more.*

Night of the Dead

for Carolyn

Costumed in the weight of living,
they walk the streets in shadows,
and something in them surviving
the first frost grows restless.

The leaves are stilled in an instant.
The air as moist as dead breath
scratches at the face. A distant
voice calls and goes unanswered.

I take her small frightened hand
in mine as the painted personae pass;
a voice of reason tries to understand
what it is to go among the awakened

for one night to see the stars behind
the veil of an overshadowed moon.
I look into that pale face designed
with eyebrow pencil and rouge.

Hear the soft step of her shoes on thresholds,
the rattle of a samhain sack she holds.

If the Snows Dance

they could be saying that the wind
is alive; that the world has risen
from its grave and its dusts find

every soul desiring resurrection;
they could be saying that the stars
in all the heavens have fallen

and fallen that we may count our
blessings one by one until they scream
their ice-bound plenty and shower

us with the starlight of a providential dream;
they could be saying here is God's eye
and it is blind from believing the mean

truth of mankind, and wondering why
there is so little peace in so many hearts;
they could be saying that the sky

is the kingdom of uncertainty that starts
the engine of faith in perpetual motion
where love is the sum of all its parts;

look long and hard at this dark ocean,
and put the sky back together,
the broken phrases of explanation

spoken on a child's tongue that has never
tasted the body of blessing in cold weather.

Wind

in memory of John O'Riordan

*The wind bloweth where it liketh, and thou hearest the sound
thereof, but cannot tell whence it cometh, and whither it
goeth: so is everyone that is born of the Spirit.*

John 3:7-8

1)

Whispered by my ears at graveside,
sang low in the temporal lobes
and droned a thawing farewell.

The casket had been so heavy,
weighed heavily like a reply
I had been impatient to hear —

the sobs, the secret words spoken,
were drowned by the March air...
and my ears deafened, useless

and humming like a Chorus
said simply, *listen to tragedy.*
So what is life but final roses?

I asked God for an answer
but He took away my hearing
just in the breath of time.

2)

Let us say a prayer for the departed.
Heads bowed. The muddy ground
sucks at our shoes. The words started
to flow but the air in them found

more air and slowly they meant
nothing. It will soon be spring.
Halfway through with head bent
I opened my eyes almost expecting

to see the hand of an angel
resting upon the shoulders of
the mourners; but it is all
sunlight, all fragments of love

like a face in a broken mirror
trying to retrace its beauty.
I cannot look. I see another
in front of me, there to do duty

to the dead, to suffer the silence
that is said in simple disbelief.
And tomorrow, the naked solace
will answer silence with grief.

3)

It would be easy to believe if it
could be easy to see God in the dark

expensive limousines, in the neat
arrangements of gladiolas and stark

roses torn from their summer somewhere
distant and unfamiliar, in the hands

reaching out for comfort, in the care
with which the attendant stands

in his mourning suit and somber face
trying to restrain the monotony

of his daily routine in this place
where the dead are kept far away

from the city, its traffic and streets
where the drivers argue over a place

to park their cars, and the sheets
of financial reports that grace

the desktops of glass towers...
it would be so easy to believe

if we had been given the powers
to understand God's love and relieve

us of the wonder and worry faith
begs us to embrace. These tears

I kiss on solemn faces, this death
that pits small wills against great fears

comes without rainbows or promises,
and what is miraculous is the way

we simply stand there, coats, dresses
blowing in the wind as we pray,

knowing not whether we are heard
or loved beyond in the eternal

silence of God's kingdom, but lured
to praise the breath that made it all.

St. Stephen's Green at Sunrise

Everything on the green was frosted white —
trees, stone statues of fallen soldiers,
an iron bench where a day before might
have slept a ragged body; if he was there

now, would wake to find himself dressed
in gauze hoar laid on everything,
like furniture in a house left to the test
of cold hours, alone and waiting.

This too is waiting: each channeling vein
in each leaf is traced in delicate line
each dark footprint an intrusion
into the stillness too holy, too still to define

in words. Now, before the anxious city
wakes, before careless dustmen and taxis
toss the world like some worn old paltry
object that has no purpose, remember these

things, this moment in the risen sun
when the world without end was innocent
and the clockwork pain of time had not begun
that instant before perfection was spent.

Carry it in you, carry it like a pearl,
this place sewn in the memory's coarse hem.
If anyone asks is there song left in the world
the answer is *no*, unless you love them.

Bruce Meyer is author of the *The Golden Thread*, poetry collections *The Open Room, Radio Silence* and *The Presence* and the short story collection *Goodbye Mr. Spalding*. He co-edited *The Selected Poems of Frank Prewett* with Barry Callaghan. A frequent broadcaster on CBC's *This Morning* on 'the Great Books,' he is Director of the Writing and Literature program at the University of Toronto School of Continuing Studies.